Economically Developing Countries

Malaysia

Jonathan Rowell

HODDER
Wayland

an imprint of Hodder Children's Books

Economically Developing Countries

Brazil   **India**

China   **Malaysia**

Egypt   **Vietnam**

Cover picture: Petronas Towers
Title page: Mount Kinabalu in Sabah. Breathtaking scenery like this needs to be preserved.
Contents page: A group of Malay children play together in a park.

Picture acknowledgements: All the photographs in this book were taken by Jimmy Holmes except: Allan Flachs 41, 43; Ole Steen Hansen 3, 4, 17; Topham Picture Point *Cover.* Illustrations by Peter Bull.

Editor: Katie Orchard
Designers: Mark Whitchurch and Malcolm Walker

Text copyright © 2001 Hodder Wayland
Volume copyright © 2001 Hodder Wayland

First published in 1996 by Wayland Publishers Ltd.
This edition updated and reprinted in 2001 by Hodder Wayland,
an imprint of Hodder Children's Books.

British Library Cataloguing in Publication Data
Rowell, Jonathan
   Malaysia: a study of an economically developing country. - (Economically developing countries)
   1. Malaysia – Economic conditions – Juvenile literature
   2. Malaysia – Social conditions – Juvenile literature
   I. Title
   959.5'054

ISBN 0 7502 3401 6

Printed and bound by G. Canale & C.S.pA., Turin, Italy.

Hodder Children's Books
A Division of Hodder Headline Limited
338 Euston Road, London NW1 3BH

Contents

Introduction

Malaysia is a complex country because it is made up of two parts and is divided into three separate territories. West Malaysia is a long finger of land known as the Malay Peninsula, surrounded by the South China Sea. East Malaysia consists of Sabah and Sarawak, and forms a strip along the northern coast of the island of Borneo, 700 km across the South China Sea. The many states of the Malay Peninsula, along with Sabah and Sarawak, form the Federation of Malaysia.

Malaysia is a country of contrasts. In East Malaysia, indigenous peoples still live mainly in the forests, whereas in West Malaysia, modern cities are common and the people's lifestyles are similar to those in Europe or the USA.

Malaysia's position at the heart of Asia, means that it lies on the major trading routes of the Asian continent. This has led to a mixed and varied population in which ethnic Malays live alongside Chinese and Indian people, as well as other indigenous peoples.

THE MALAYSIAN FLAG

The Malaysian flag has been in use since independence was gained from Britain in 1963. The fourteen stripes and the fourteen points on the star, which resemble the roof of the national mosque in Kuala Lumpur, represent the original fourteen Malaysian states. When Singapore left the union in 1965, the extra point and stripe were left to stand for the capital city, Kuala Lumpur. The crescent alongside the star is a sign of Islam, the official religion. The yellow is the official colour of the monarchy, the blue reminds people of the influence of British colonial rule, and the red and white are Malaysia's traditional colours.

In central Kuala Lumpur new high-rise office blocks tower over old colonial buildings – a relic of Malaysia's past.

Area:	329,758 km^2
Official Language:	Malay (*Bahasa Melayu*)
Population:	22.2 million
Population Density:	65 persons per km^2
Capital:	Kuala Lumpur
Currency:	Malaysian Dollar, or *Ringgit*
Official Religion:	Islam
Independence Gained:	1963
Highest mountain:	Mount Kinabalu, 4,094 m

Source: *United Nations, 2000*

Above *The thirteen states of Malaysia.*

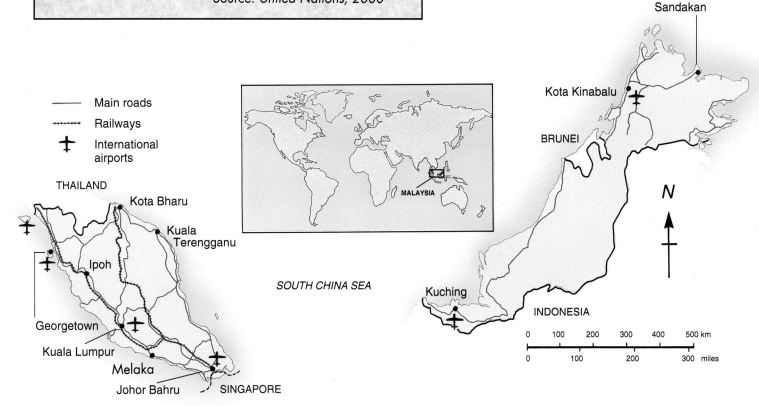

Malays make up about half of the population in Malaysia and they hold a position of advantage in Malaysian society. A New Economic Policy (NEP) which was first introduced in the early 1970s, benefits Malays by helping them to find work, giving them special rights to own land and recommending that secondary education is taught in *Bahasa Melayu*, the mother tongue.

Malaysia is a rapidly developing country. It has held the position of being one of the fastest-growing economies in Asia since 1988. The economy was once ruled by the production of tin, rubber and timber, but now manufactured goods, such as computer disc drives and cars, account for two-thirds of Malaysia's exports. Malaysia has developed so quickly that economists no longer consider it a developing country, but a newly industrialized one.

Development in Malaysia must be carefully planned if it is to continue successfully. In the late 1990s, Southeast Asia entered a time of economic troubles, but Malaysia suffered less than many nations in the region. Full industrialization by 2020 is Malaysia's most ambitious target to date.

***Opposite** In Kelantan, on the Malay Peninsula, a Malay farmer returns from his day's work in the rice fields. These productive flat plains contrast with the mountains inland.*

SOCIAL INDICATORS OF DEVELOPMENT	
Life expectancy	72
Under-five infant mortality rate	10 per 1,000 live births
Percentage of adults who can read and write	86.4
Percentage of children who attend secondary school	64
	Source: *United Nations Human Development Report, 2000*

***Below** Kota Kinabalu is the state capital of Sabah, situated at the tip of East Malaysia.*

1786	The British occupy Penang, an island off the north coast of Malaysia, and set up a colony ruled from India
1896	Selangor, Negeri Sembilan and Pahang become the Federated Malay States (FMS)
1919	'British Malaya' formed as all the peninsula states join together
1930	Malaysian Communist Party (MCP) formed
1942	British Malaya and Singapore are occupied by the Japanese
1948	The MCP who fought against the Japanese during the War try to end British colonial rule to gain independence
1955	The Malaysian and Malayan Chinese political parties call for independence
1957	Malaya achieves independence (*merdeka*). First Prime Minister Tengku Abdul Rahman appointed
1963	Singapore, Sabah and Sarawak join Malaya to form Malaysia
1965	Singapore and Malaysia separate. As most of the population of Singapore were Chinese, they did not want to be ruled by Malays. Malays also feared the influence of Singapore because of its high Chinese population. The split therefore benefited both Singapore and Malaysia
1981	Dato Sri Dr Mahathir Mohammed becomes Malaysia's fourth Prime Minister and still holds that office
1996	Economic crisis hits Southeast Asia and slows progress on building projects.

Land and the environment

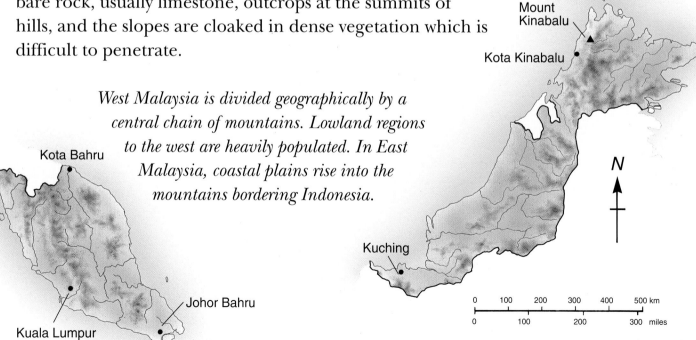

WEST MALAYSIA

In West Malaysia, a central chain of mountains divides the country into its geographical regions. The mountains separate fertile lowlands to the west from a narrow belt on the eastern coast. Human activity on the western plains has transformed the landscape. Both the rural areas and the towns and cities are heavily populated. There are many Malay villages surrounded by rice fields. Rubber and oil palm estates alongside tin mines help to make this an industrial zone. The population is a mixture of Malay, Chinese and Indian peoples.

East and south of the mountains, the second lowland region has a different character. This area is less developed, poorer, more rural and less densely populated. The majority of people living in this area are Malays, whose activities are based upon small-scale farming and fishing.

Few people live in the mountains because they consist of bare rock, usually limestone, outcrops at the summits of hills, and the slopes are cloaked in dense vegetation which is difficult to penetrate.

In the hot climate, clouds rise above the thick, mountainous forests following an afternoon rainstorm.

West Malaysia is divided geographically by a central chain of mountains. Lowland regions to the west are heavily populated. In East Malaysia, coastal plains rise into the mountains bordering Indonesia.

Kota Bahru

Kuala Lumpur

Johor Bahru

Mount Kinabalu

Kota Kinabalu

Kuching

N

| 0 | 100 | 200 | 300 | 400 | 500 km |

| 0 | 100 | 200 | 300 miles |

8

Malaysia accounts for over half the world's exports of tropical timber compared to 27 per cent from Indonesia and only a small percentage from Brazil.

Logging does not use the same sustainable methods today as deforestation in the past. The agriculture of the forest people resulted in trees being cleared. However, the population was low and the periods when cleared areas were left to regrow were long.

Tropical timber is a valuable resource. To supply the developed world's demand for timber, a huge rise in commercial logging has taken place. Because the demand is so high, there is no time to let the old forests regrow and instead they are replaced by fast-growing trees that damage the soils. The complex root systems of the old forest trees are gone so they no longer hold the soil together. Once the soil is washed away, the old forests can never grow again on this land.

Even so, the future of tropical logging is threatened by competition from cooler climates and the possibility that the timber may eventually run out.

'My husband drives a truck like this which takes logs from the interior of Sabah through to the sawmill. He is often away for weeks at a time and we never get a chance to see him, so we came out here to visit. We are quite lucky though because this is a good job and he is well paid. We live in the town in our own house with the luxuries that we want.'
– Winnie Chan (logger's wife).

EAST MALAYSIA

In East Malaysia, the coastal plains are characterized by mangrove swamps that rise into mountains on the border with Indonesia. Flowing across the states to the coast are large rivers, such as the River Rajang in Sarawak and the River Kinabatangan in Sabah. In East Malaysia, the water has worn away the rock and huge caves have appeared. The cave systems at Niah and Mulu in Sarawak are still being discovered but some, such as the Sarawak Chamber, are the biggest in the world. In Sabah, Mount Kinabalu is the highest mountain between the Himalayas and New Guinea.

Logging means that Winnie, pictured here with her daughter, can live in a way she might never have dreamed of when she was young.

9

The Endau Rompin National Park

Although 7,460 km² of forest in Malaysia is protected, there has only ever been one national park, the Taman Negara, situated on the Malay Peninsula. To protect more land, the government chose to conserve the Endau Rompin forest which covers the border between Johor and Pahang, since it was one of the last stretches of undisturbed forest in the south.

There was already a wildlife sanctuary on the Johor side which, among many other animal species, protected the endangered Sumatran Rhinoceros. The original idea was to preserve 2,023 km² of land. This was to include a 919 km² fully protected core and the remaining 1,104 km² was going to be managed as a forest reserve. However, in 1977, it became known that the Pahang state government had approved plans to log 120 km² of the core area and the logging had already begun. The Malaysian people protested and finally the state gave in, refusing to issue any more logging licences. However, 52 km² of forest had already been cleared.

In 1980, a National Parks Act was passed, which meant that Endau Rompin achieved full status as a conservation area. However, the state refused to hand over the land to the Malaysian government.

An angry public, helped by the Malayan Nature Society, continued to press for change. Finally, in 1988, Endau Rompin became a park without the state losing control of its land. Although the park protects a smaller area than was originally hoped for (930 km² rather than 2,023 km²) it remains a victory for conservation.

East Malaysia is less developed than the Malay Peninsula. There are few towns and the infrastructure is only just beginning to expand. Great emphasis is placed on primary production, such as agriculture, timber and oil. Despite its isolation (it takes two and a half hours to fly from Kuala Lumpur in West Malaysia to Kota Kinabalu in Sabah) East Malaysia is of great economic importance to the whole of the country.

The River Kinabatangan in Sabah.

The clouds before the storm are a daily sight in many parts of Malaysia.

CLIMATE

The tropical climate of Malaysia is characterized by high temperatures and humidity all year round. It rains throughout the year on 150–200 days, but this rarely lasts all of each day. In West Malaysia, the wet season occurs on the west coast from September to December and, on the east coast, where it is more pronounced, between October and February. In East Malaysia, the rain is even heavier and flooding is common.

Temperatures rarely fall below 20 °C even at night and usually climb to 30 °C or higher during the day.

CLIMATE			
KUALA LUMPUR		LABUAN, SABAH	
Month	Average rainfall (mm)	Month	Average rainfall (mm)
Jan	158	Jan	112
Feb	201	Feb	117
March	259	March	150
April	292	April	297
May	224	May	345
June	130	June	351
July	99	July	318
Aug	163	Aug	297
Sept	218	Sept	417
Oct	249	Oct	465
Nov	259	Nov	419
Dec	191	Dec	285

Source: World Weather Guide, 1990

11

FLORA AND FAUNA

Examples of some of the most ancient forest in the world can be found in Malaysia. It is home to one of the most varied plant communities in existence and an enormous number of animal species. Over 2,000 types of tree and 200 kinds of palm have been recorded and, in the canopy high above the forest floor, many insects remain unidentified. Some of the most bizarre insects resemble other natural objects, such as branches or flowers, as a disguise. On Mount Kinabalu, the slopes are covered by almost 1,000 orchids and pitcher-plants, so called because their leaves form sacks that can hold liquids to trap insects. The world's largest flower, rafflesia, originated in Sabah. The rafflesia blooms quickly and is rarely spotted, which is surprising as the flower can grow to 3 m in width. Despite its beauty, the rafflesia smells of rotting meat to attract flies that will pollinate the flower before it rapidly withers.

The rain forest, however, is under threat from logging. Timber production is vital to the Malaysian economy and so the felling of trees to be cut into logs continues. This results in the deforestation of large areas. To protect the environment, a balance between logging rights and conservation has been struck. In 1935, the Taman Negara National Park was created. A smaller area than ever has been set aside for tree clearance and many trees have been replanted in zones that have already been cleared. However, the actual area of forest available for logging has already been dramatically reduced.

Clouds surround the summit of Mount Kinabalu, in Sabah, which is 4,094 m high.

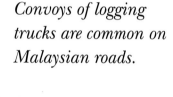

Convoys of logging trucks are common on Malaysian roads.

12

No one is certain where the name Kinabalu comes from. It may be derived from the local dialect, Dusun, *Aki Nabalu* meaning 'sacred place of the dead'. But the indigenous peoples, the Kadazan, have another explanation. An emperor of China had heard that the mountain was home to a fabulous pearl and sent his three sons to find it and bring it back to him. The mountain was protected by a dragon, who drove the first two sons away. While they made their escape, the third son managed to snatch the jewel, but decided to remain in Borneo. He married and, after raising a family, chose to return to China to take his place on the throne. He promised that he would come back for his wife, but he never did. So, in despair, she decided to climb the mountain to pray that he would come back for her. However, she died before she reached the summit of the mountain, so the Kadazan believe that Mount Kinabalu was named after her since *Kina* means 'China' and *balu* means 'widow'.

Yassan Sekambeng explains the importance of preserving scenic places, such as Mount Kinabalu.

'For over ten years I have been working on this mountain. This place means a lot to me, although it does not mean the same to me as it does to my parents. My folks used to think that the mountain had a spirit, and that we would go there when we died. But to me, it has a more realistic meaning. Many guides and porters earn a living by working with the tourists here. We enjoy our work and respect the wildlife and forest. But more people have to learn that we must preserve these special places.'
– Yassan Sekambeng, Kinabalu mountain guide.

Transport

In Malaysia, much has been done to improve the communications network. A good communications network by road, rail, air and water is essential to the development of any country, but the geography of Malaysia, with its central mountain ranges, makes it a difficult task.

ROADS

In Malaysia, many roads began as logging tracks, or routes that led to rubber plantations and tin mines. Now these have been upgraded, lengthened and joined to form a modern transport network. The road system of any country is a good marker of its development and, at the same time, helps the districts through which roads are built to grow. Roads are mainly concentrated in the industrialized western region. Here, the north-south highway from Butterworth to Johor Bahru, via Kuala Lumpur, links the main towns.

Above A traffic jam during the rush hour in Kuala Lumpur. This scene is repeated in all Malaysia's major towns.

Left A road worker repairs a drain at the side of a modern city road.

As the road network has expanded, more remote states have become easier to reach. A 6 km bridge now links Penang to the mainland, and this has helped the island to attract industry. Even the central mountain chain in West Malaysia has been crossed. In the far north, close to the Thailand border, a winding road joins the west and east coasts. It is now surfaced along its entire length and has improved access to the traditional state of Kelantan, where strict Islamic law is observed, alcohol is banned and women are often veiled.

Sabah is the best example in Malaysia of how the rate of development depends on communications. In 1985, roads between the major towns were still mostly dirt tracks. By 1995, all routes even as far as Tawau in the south-east were tarred, making journeys shorter and more comfortable. As a consequence, in the same ten-year period, the number of people owning cars tripled.

The main north-south highway on the Malay Peninsula is dual carriageway for much of its length.

To avoid congestion, which slows traffic during peak hours to walking pace, a new Light Rail Transit system (LRT) has opened in Kuala Lumpur. The system operates electric trains and has been running since August 1995.

The first reactions of Kuala Lumpur's residents were mixed. For the first few days, all journeys were free and the system was well used. But some still complained because it did not go near enough to their house or, when fares were introduced, they would not be able to afford them. Indeed, the number of people travelling on the service did drop once fares were charged. So, many were only using it because it was free, but there were others who continued to use and pay for the new trains. They enjoyed the extra comfort and speed of the service. Some said they would leave their cars at home and were looking forward to the growth of the service.

A train operator on Kuala Lumpur's new LRT prepares for his trip to the suburbs.

'The new rolling stock of the railway has really changed the way people think about the train system. I've seen so many people start to commute by train and leave their cars at home. It's so much more efficient. The roads are so busy these days, with long traffic jams, and it's expensive to find a place to park in the city. As soon as the new LRT elevated train system is completed the situation will get even better.' – LRT train operator.

Below Parts of central Kuala Lumpur are so congested that tracks for the new railway have been built above the roads.

RAILWAYS

Like the original road network, the railways were first built in colonial times. The main railway line runs north-south through the western region of the Malay Peninsula.

A secondary line links Kota Bahru in the north-east of West Malaysia to Kuala Lumpur, and passes through the middle of the central mountain chain where there are no roads. Small-scale industry and some settlements have appeared along the route of this so-called 'Jungle Railway'.

In contrast, a new railway, linking Kuala Lumpur and its suburbs, started operating services in the summer of 1995. The new Light Rail Transit was built to ease congestion on the city's roads.

AIR AND WATER TRANSPORT

Even though it is not a big country, it will always be difficult and time-consuming to reach parts of Malaysia by land. The problem is overcome by using other forms of transport. A reliable air service has been introduced and most settlements larger than a village, have an airstrip. Malaysia Airlines (MAS) provide daily flights between most towns and cities.

A Boeing 737 being boarded for take off. Malaysia Airlines has the biggest fleet of this type in Asia.

At smaller locations you can expect to disembark on to a runway tarmac, from a small aircraft, with all your belongings and cargo. This contrasts sharply with the international airport, Sepang, which is modern, air-conditioned and spacious. In the late 1990s, Subang, Malaysia's first international airport, became overcrowded. A new airport opened at Sepang in 1998.

Rivers are also used in places where they offer the only practical means of communication. In Sarawak, for example, the people are dependent upon river transport. Inland waterways are navigable deep into the interior. Fast launch boats, called *expres*, which can travel up to 60 kph, ferry goods and passengers to markets further downstream or on the coast.

For a country surrounded by sea, marine transport is very important. As the number of foreign markets supplied by Malaysian products grows, the goods coming in and going out of Malaysia increases. To deal with this extra trade, international ports such as those at Melaka and Butterworth are constantly developing.

A crew at Sibu wait for cargo, which their fast launch boat will carry upriver into the interior of Sarawak.

The many peoples of Malaysia

Two things characterize Malaysian society: the diversity of its ethnic groups and its location at the centre of trading routes between India and China. Malaysia's peoples include Malay, Chinese, Tamil (Indian) and indigenous groups. In West Malaysia, indigenous groups are referred to as *Orang Asli*, and in East Malaysia, *Dayaks*.

The most important distinction in Malaysian society is between the Muslim Malays and the Chinese. Although the Malays are the largest group, they only amount to about 55 per cent of the total population in West Malaysia, and even less in East Malaysia. Malays are called *bumiputera*. They choose Islam as their only religion and follow Malay culture in all its forms. Their official language, *Bahasa Melayu*, is also the official national language and is spoken in Malaysian business and education. Malays are generally country people rather than town people.

For the Chinese, the coffee-shop is more than just somewhere to eat and drink, it is also a place to socialize and read the paper.

'The Chinese community has been in the Taiping area of Malaysia for over 150 years. We came here originally to work the tin mines and do labouring jobs. We have our traditions still and this old-style coffee shop is little changed over the years.'
– Mr Ho Kok Liong, Chinese coffee shop.

As Malaysia's industry has grown, the number of people moving to cities to find jobs and improve their standard of living has increased. When industry stopped growing, during the recession of the early 1980s, for example, the movement to towns slowed because there were fewer new jobs. People have always been attracted to big cities.

To prevent the overcrowding that this leads to, the Malaysian government has encouraged the development of smaller towns in Kelantan, Kedah, Perlis and Pahang. As this has not stopped the flow of people to the largest cities, such as Kuala Lumpur, new settlements have been built on the edges of these areas. Services and work are provided locally to keep people away from the centre. Over the past twenty years, more than fifty new towns have been planned or are being developed.

Although there were Chinese people in Malaysia from early times, their numbers greatly increased during the nineteenth century.

Most came from the southern provinces of China and now make up about a third of the population of Malaysia. Hakkas, Hokkiens, Teochews and Cantonese are some of the many dialects spoken.

The Chinese have kept their religious and cultural practices, and rarely spend any time socially with people who are not Chinese. Most Chinese people live in towns and cities, where they control the majority of businesses.

Islam is the national religion of Malaysia. Malay men pray at a mosque.

'My father moved here to Malaysia when I was still young. I suppose he was looking for a better life and followed my other relatives who had been in Malaysia for some time. Business is good here and there are plenty of business opportunities in such a rapidly growing economy. Things are changing so quickly here now.'
– Miss Thavaman, Indian trader.

Many Indians in Malaysia are merchants. An Indian shopkeeper displays the materials she sells.

The third major group, the Indians, account for 10 per cent of the population. They came to work on the plantations for British colonists around the beginning of the twentieth century. They are mainly Tamils and now live in the larger towns on the west coast of West Malaysia.

Small and scattered indigenous groups together make up only about 5 per cent of the population. In West Malaysia, the *Orang Asli*, the 'Original People', consist of three main groups – the Negritos, Senoi and Jakun. Living mainly in the mountains, they work as farmers or collect forest products. Traditional shifting cultivation has been abandoned as they have become more integrated into Malay society.

In East Malaysia, the mix of non-Muslim peoples is more complicated. Together, the ethnic groups are called *Dayaks*, but they consist of more than 200 different groups. In Sarawak, the Iban is the most common, followed by the Bidayuh. The majority live in communal dwellings called longhouses, that are built on the banks of the great rivers. These are the people who are directly affected by deforestation because they rely upon the habitat which is being destroyed for their survival. The Penan suffer most as they continue to live a hunter-gatherer existence.

ETHNIC AND RELIGIOUS DIVERSITY IN MALAYSIA

ETHNIC GROUP	Percentage of population
Malay	50%
Chinese	35%
Indigenous groups	5%
Indian	10%
Other	4%

RELIGIONS	Percentage of population
Islam	50%
Buddhism	6%
Chinese faiths	25%
Hinduism	7%
Christianity	6%
Other	5%

21

'I'm from the Philippines originally, but we've lived in Sandakan, almost in this exact spot, for over twenty years now. I wouldn't live anywhere else. We have such a great community spirit, and such a mixed bunch of folks. Indonesians. Malays, Chinese, and we all get on together.'
– Aida Javines, inhabitant of a stilt house.

In Sabah, Kadazans form the major ethnic group, alongside the Murat and Sulu. Traditionally, the Kadazan are farmers, but many have now moved to the towns to find work. In the past, the Sulu people were known to be pirates. However, it is now thought to be illegal

Stilt houses provide accommodation for the many immigrants in Sabah.

The impact of development on indigenous groups of Sarawak

'We aren't quite sure who is cutting our forests and who is going to flood our land. But we know they live in towns, where rich people are getting richer while we poor people are losing what little we have.'
– Iban statement.

Sibu, 60 km from the mouth of the Rajang River in Sarawak, is a point where traditional and modern worlds meet. It is a Chinese town, where boats on the wide river compete for trade. The streets are characterized by *Dayak* people, particularly the Iban, who can be identified by their elaborate tattoos. In years gone by, the Iban would not have travelled this far, but many have been forced off their land by development projects. Now they come to towns such as Sibu to find work. Other indigenous groups pass through Sibu on their way to Kuching, the capital of Sarawak. They hope to find tourists who want to visit and stay in one of the *Dayak* longhouses. Tourist trips to longhouses are set to become a major source of income for communities who live in this traditional way.

The different indigenous groups have never lived entirely without contact with each other or the outside world. They would meet to trade or to fight wars, but remained independent and self-sufficient. The people exploited the rain forest with an economy based on shifting

Even when the Iban are forced to move from their homelands, they build new longhouses.

immigrants from the Philippines or Indonesia who are responsible. They live in the coastal towns of Sandakan, Lahad Datu and Tawau.

Even though there is a great variety of peoples in Malaysia, the country is underpopulated. Unlike elsewhere in the world, where overpopulation is often the reason for the slow pace of development, the Malaysian economy will not continue to grow without an increase in the number of people. People are the fuel that help economies to grow. Without enough people to fill the jobs in an increasingly expanding economy, growth will stop.

cultivation. They would eat root crops in addition to forest sago (a cereal) and, where conditions and soils were suitable, cultivated wet rice.

This traditional way of life is, however, slowly being destroyed. This is because the forests are ideal locations for hydroelectric power schemes and their timber is vital for the economy of Malaysia. These activities use land which the Dayaks have always had access to, and suitable protected areas are not being set aside for the tribes.

'We are all from the Iban ethnic group here, and this is our traditional way to live. Sharing one long building helps us stay together as a community. The materials and construction of our longhouse are new because we had to move from the valley, which is now underwater after they built the hydroelectric dam.' – **Mr Nyambar Nyelang, Longhouse.**

For the indigenous peoples, who continue to live in the remote regions, signs of the influence of change are everywhere. The longhouse may well have been built using ancient methods, but now banks of televisions line the inside. They have the electricity to turn them on, but the TV signal was never set up to reach that far, so when the television is switched on, the screen remains blank.

Agriculture and natural resources

Malaysia is blessed with many natural resources that have helped the country to develop. They fall into three basic categories – agricultural, mineral and energy.

AGRICULTURE

The agricultural sector was once the main source of Malaysia's growth but, as the economy and industry have grown, it has become less important. However, its decline is partly due to the type of agriculture that is practised.

Over the past twenty years, government policy has favoured farmers with smallholdings. These are small areas of agricultural land that are farmed. The farmers of these areas own and live on the land. Despite being an uneconomical way to farm, Malays were encouraged to stay on the land with financial aid from the government. The government aimed to help the poor, by giving Malays a greater share of the country's wealth, but it was not an efficient way to get the best from the land. At times, for example, a Malay

When sections of forest are cleared they are often replaced by large estate farms.

NATURAL RESOURCES PRODUCTION (millions of ringgit)				
	1996	1997	1998	1999
Palm oil	4,546	4,901	4,644	5,922
Rubber	2,069	1,868	1,688	1,472
Livestock, forestry and fishing	11,274	11,242	11,081	10,604
Mining and quarrying	14,040	14,306	14,425	13,973

Source: *IMF, 2000*

farmer would spend more money growing cash crops, such as rubber, oil palm or cocoa, than they would make when their produce was sold. Discouraged by the small amounts of money that they were getting back from their investment, farmers grew rice, vegetables or tropical fruits instead. With these crops they could at least feed their families and any that was left over could be sold at the local market.

Many decided that farming had become too much of a risk and left the countryside altogether. They moved to towns, to work in jobs that offered more security and were better paid. In response, the government supported a return to farming large estates. Plantations were large enough to buy machinery and fertilizers that small farmers could never afford. They made more money because cash crops are better suited to large-scale production. Overall, costs were also reduced by taking away the workers and replacing them with machinery. This helped to financially protect the plantation owners when prices for agricultural produce were low because salaries did not have to be paid to the workers.

An oil palm plantation in Sabah, East Malaysia. Oil palm plantations cover huge areas of land.

The palm oil industry

The lasting memories of many who visit Malaysia are the bitter smells as they drive through the countryside, the furry, pine cone-like objects they swerve to avoid in the road and smoke billowing from the middle of a plantation. These are all due to Malaysia's most important agricultural product, palm oil. Crude palm oil (CPO) is pressed from the fleshy outer part of a palm fruit. These fruits grow in bunches of between 800 and 1,000. Two years after they have reached the plantation, the oil palm begins producing enough oil to sell commercially. The oil can be harvested from the palm for about thirty years, after which it becomes too tall. Each tree will produce between five and fifteen bunches of palm fruit per year and the average yield is about 3.8 tonnes of fruit per 10,000 m^2.

Once harvested, the fruit must be ground rapidly since it deteriorates quickly. Palm oil mills are always located on or near a plantation and they produce CPO, which can then be refined further to make industrial products such as soap, or foodstuffs such as cooking oil. Palm fruits also produce palm kernels from which palm kernel oil is extracted. This is very different from CPO and is classed as a different product.

Palm oil fruit arrives at the mill on a plantation in Sabah.

The success or failure of a crop depends on its selling price and the cost of growing it. Malaysia was once the world's leading natural rubber producer, but has recently been overtaken by Thailand and Indonesia. It costs less to produce rubber in these countries because machinery is cheaper and labour costs are lower. The agricultural sector has responded in several ways. Most local workers have moved to towns, so foreign workers are employed instead – up to 70 per cent on some plantations. Owners have converted their lands to produce better-paying crops.

In addition, the sap of the tree can be fermented to make alcohol. So the bitter smells and the billowing smoke are a small price to pay for such a diverse and profitable plant.

The success of palm oil can be traced back to the 1950s. Malaysia's economic dependence on rubber began to decline as estate owners looked for another crop to replace it. The infrastructure of plantations already existed on rubber estates and the government allowed grants for replanting palm fruits instead.

As palm oil made more money it expanded rapidly, and Malaysia is now the world's largest producer. However, it faces stiff competition from its neighbouring countries, Indonesia and Thailand, but has found new markets, such as China, which help to protect its number one position.

'There is no dispute really. Palm oil is a very successful crop. It's amazing just how many everyday products our oil goes into. It is possible that in the future we may even be able to use palm oil in motor engines. With a steady price and increasing demand, the future looks good, and we have so much empty land out here that can be planted with palms.' – Mr Chong Min Sang, Plantation Manager.

A plantation manager checks the palm oil fruit after harvesting.

Palm oil is a favourite as its market price remains high. Many owners have even sold their properties for building and leisure development.

Emphasis has also been placed on diversification and branching out into agricultural-related production. Palm oil, for instance, which was once just sold in its raw state, is now being refined and sold as oils and fats. The rubber sector has also expanded and now makes gloves and condoms.

Even though the importance of agriculture in the economy is declining, this area still employs 18.4 per cent of Malaysian workers.

MINERALS

Tin was once the most important part of the Malaysian economy. It is also the most saleable raw material which the country is most well known for. In 1983, Malaysia was producing more than 60,000 tonnes of tin each year. Ten years later, extraction fell below 10,000 tonnes. Whether tin is mined or not depends on the international market price. In 1983, the metal was fetching between US$12–14 per kilogram on the Kuala Lumpur tin market. In 1993, it was down to US$3.75. Low prices have forced mines such as the Sungai Lembing – once one of the world's biggest single sources of tin – to be abandoned and reopened several times during the twentieth century. At the moment, the mine is still extracting ore, but only in amounts that cover the costs of keeping the mine in a workable state.

An old tin mine in Malaysia. In the years since tin was last extracted, vegetation has begun to grow over the mine.

ENERGY

In 1992, a power cut in West Malaysia left the peninsula without electricity for several days. This was because industrial growth had caused the demand for energy to become greater than the amount being produced. The government immediately began a programme of increasing its energy production. To speed up the process and find the money to finance the improvements, part of the national electricity board, Tenaga Nasional Berhad (TNB), was sold to the private sector. It became the largest company on the Kuala Lumpur Stock Exchange.

Independent energy producers are now building gas-fuelled power stations. They will buy gas from the state-owned oil and gas company, Petronas, and sell the power to TNB. TNB is now responsible for transmitting and supplying electricity via the national grid, which is the network of power lines that run between the major power stations.

'I was born in 1935 and the big tin mines around Taiping closed in the 1950s. My father came here from Thailand to work in the mines in about 1888. Now the industry is almost dead. Most of the mines have even been filled in now and houses and shops built on the land.' – **Mr Lim-Chene Hoon, tin miner.**

A former tin miner remembers how important, at one time, tin was to Malaysia.

THE IMPACT OF THE OIL INDUSTRY IN KERTEH

Before the arrival of the state-owned oil company, Petronas, Kerteh was a small fishing village on the east coast of West Malaysia. Petronas is exploiting the oil offshore and where, at night, Kerteh used to be dark and quiet, it is now brightly lit and buzzing with activity. The area has become characterized by its industrial skyline, and these dramatic changes have had an impact on the population. As a result, two different communities have developed: migrant employees of Petronas, who live in modern housing estates provided by the company, and the locals who still live in their traditional homes. The petroleum people care little about the area in which they live and locals are unsure of what the future holds.

Malaysia has the resources to be self-sufficient in energy. It has oil and gas reserves off the eastern coast of the peninsula and in the states of Sarawak and Sabah. The generation of hydroelectric power (HEP) is also becoming more important as Malaysia looks for other ways of supplying power. However, HEP schemes have caused arguments and disruption. Indiginous groups are moved off land where they have lived for centuries and the reservoirs flood areas that might be put to better use. However, such schemes could make up the lack of power, or even lead to Malaysia having a surplus of electricity.

29

The Bakun Dam

In the heart of the Sarawak jungle, construction on an HEP dam began in 1996. The Bakun Dam will be the third largest in Asia. Almost 700 km² of prime forest will be flooded – an area larger than Singapore – and 6,000 people, mainly from the Penan and Kenyah peoples, will have to be moved. But the power this HEP project will generate – 2,400 mw – is not for Sarawak, but West Malaysia.

The electricity will be transmitted by 670 km of overhead cables in Sarawak, and then through 600 km of cable beneath the South China Sea. This will be the longest underwater cable ever laid. In the process, up to 25 per cent of the power may be lost. When complete, the dam will stretch 204 m across the Rajang River.

Faced with environmental concerns, the first plans were scrapped in 1990. However, because the country needs the energy to sustain its industrial growth, the plans were later revived.

Controversy surrounds both the study of the environmental impact that the project will cause and the dam itself. The project has now been divided into three phases: the building of a reservoir (Phase 1), the building of the dam (Phase 2) and the laying of the cable (Phase 3). Phase 1 has been approved, but Phases 2 and 3 have yet to be accepted. In the late 1990s, work on the dam stopped when money ran low as a result of the economic crisis in Southeast Asia.

Some people welcome the project because it is expected that the dam will create new roads, new jobs and improved opportunities and communications. For example, the town of Belaga, just below the site, can only be reached by a twice-weekly flight or seven-hour boat trip at present. However, the suggestion of chains of smaller dams, rather than a single large dam, is favoured.

A small dam in Sarawak. This dam will be dwarfed by the vast Bakun Dam once it is completed.

A developing economy

Malaysia's economy is characterized by the exceptional growth of its manufacturing industries, the growing status of its financial markets and the amount of construction that is taking place.

Factories in Putrajaya being prepared for new businesses.

MANUFACTURING

From 1976–96, Malaysia's manufacturing industries have grown so much that they have become the largest part of the economy. In the early 1970s, 70 per cent of exports consisted of rubber and tin but, in 1994, manufactured goods accounted for 78 per cent of the total value of exports.

SECTORS OF THE ECONOMY, 1999	
	Percentage of GDP
Manufacturing	29%
Farming	9%
Trade and hotels	15%
Banking and finance	12%
Mining	7%
Transport and communications	8%
Building	3%
Other	17%

Source: *IMF, 2000*

Cars at the Proton factory awaiting export to foreign countries.

Penang – Silicon Island

Penang, an island off the north-west coast of West Malaysia, is one of the most successful states in the country, but it has been a long, hard struggle. In the 1960s, Penang was in the thick of a depression, with 16 per cent of its working population unemployed. The local authority tried to attract companies from overseas, whose businesses would employ a large number of people. By the 1990s, unemployment had dropped to below 5 per cent, but most of the workers had few skills and were poorly paid.

Unhappy with this situation, Penang has made itself into a hi-tech industrial centre based upon electronics. At first it developed electrical assembly plants, but now Penang is basing its future on the production of computer disk drives. Both Hewlett-Packard and Intel are among the increasing number of multinational computer companies who have based themselves on the island. Others have relocated on the mainland opposite Penang which is joined by the longest road bridge in Asia – the Penang Bridge. A huge number of local companies are now established on landscaped industrial parks and provide components to multinational companies.

Many of the factory units are still assembly and finishing plants for Japanese and American components, but this is changing. With help from the Penang Skills Development

'My original home is in Sarawak. I'm from the Iban ethnic group, but I have been sent to West Malaysia to receive training from an American company, which is going to build a new factory near my home town. This is a great opportunity for me because I am receiving real, on-the-job experience. With these new skills I really feel that I can move forward in the future. Expectations are high in this industry and we have to really do our best.'
– Edward Philip Ak Aga, computer disk technician, aged 23.

Corporation, local workers are now involved in research, development and processing, and are taking the place of foreign workers.

Penang's infrastructure unfortunately lags behind the growth of hi-tech production. There are regular power cuts in Penang, and the road network, although improved, is inadequate. Soaring labour costs might also lead the multinational companies to look for another Asian base, where workers are paid less. Despite these disadvantages, there remains a booming economy in Penang.

As financial services expand, banks in Malaysia will become a more common sight.

Malaysia's economic growth is due to the improvement of traditional areas of industry, such as rubber production, and the development of new industries, such as electronics. For example, Malaysia has become the world's biggest producer of computer disk drives. National industries, producing goods for the people of Malaysia, have also expanded and now sell their products abroad. Proton, the national car, for instance, is as popular overseas as it is in Malaysia.

However, a shortage of skilled labour is the result of an economy growing faster than it can train its workers. In the future, school education needs to be improved. Schools will have to prepare students for the type of work that they are now more likely to find. There is also a shortage of manual workers because of the speed of development.

Furthermore, most manufacturing exports are products made for foreign multinational companies and so the profits from such exports are rarely invested back into Malaysia's economy. However, it is hoped that, as Malaysia develops further, these problems will be overcome.

FINANCE

Malaysia's government has set out to make Kuala Lumpur one of the world's leading financial centres. In 1997, Thailand and other nations in Southeast Asia were hit by an economic crisis. However, Malaysia recovered more quickly than some other Asian nations.

Malaysia has also begun a programme of privatization. The sale of public assets raises money for the government that helps to pay for development.

33

There are more new jobs in Malaysia than there are people to fill them. Skilled labour is in short supply, but the government is taking steps to change this situation. University study has been shortened from four to three years, to enable trained people to start work earlier. The problems became worse because the government recommended that *Bahasa Melayu*, the official language, was the only language used in education. *Bahasa* does not lend itself easily to science instruction, so most Malay students study arts subjects.

The Chinese, on the other hand, tend to travel abroad and many are taught in English. When they come back to Malaysia, they are qualified to take the more technical jobs. The policy favouring the use of *Bahasa Melayu*, has somewhat backfired, and calls to revive English as a common education language have been heard.

The flow of students to foreign universities poses another problem for Malaysia. It is estimated that there are 50,000 Malaysian students studying overseas at any one time. There is, therefore, a risk that these students will not come back to work in Malaysia and, even while they are abroad, their money is spent in the country of study rather than at home. One way of stopping this drain is to bring foreign education to Malaysia, thus encouraging students to stay. London University in Britain is currently involved in talks to set up a campus in Malaysia.

CONSTRUCTION

The amount of construction being carried out in Malaysia becomes clear as you fly into Kuala Lumpur. There are hundreds of new, low- and high-cost housing developments in the western area. Suburban and new town development is matched by the Kuala Lumpur city centre project. Here the world's tallest office building, the Petronas Tower, has been built.

Cement is in short supply in Malaysia. A builder carefully protects his ration.

34

The pace of development has been greater than expected. As new houses have been erected quickly, standards have fallen. Some, which fail the rigorous building regulations, have never been occupied. The constant building work has also resulted in a cement shortage in Malaysia, and supplies and prices are now strictly controlled to prevent it from running out. Major government projects take priority, so some smaller schemes have come to a complete halt.

Rubbish litters an open sewer in Kuala Lumpur.

POLLUTION IN KUALA LUMPUR

As the number of factories in Malaysia grows, so the levels of pollution and waste increase. The people of Kuala Lumpur were once proud that their city was not like Bangkok, which is well known for its congested streets and poor air quality. Unfortunately, this is no longer the case.

In 1994, massive fires on the Indonesian islands of Sumatra and Kalimantan produced a haze that covered much of Malaysia. It trapped car exhaust and industrial fumes close to ground level. People stayed inside and schools were threatened with closure. Worse still, the pollution haze descended on Kuala Lumpur again in 1995, only this time there were no Indonesian fires to use as an excuse.

Adverse and unusual weather conditions were blamed. Malaysians in the capital care little for the reasons, but deeply regret the loss of blue skies and fresh air. One resident went as far as saying that if this is what development brought she would rather do without it.

Petronas Towers, at 452 metres high, is presently the tallest building in the world.

'We are very proud to be involved in this great project. It is a big change for an Asian country to have the tallest building in the world. Wouldn't you be proud? We have been working with other Asian partners. The Japanese helped us with one of the towers and the South Koreans helped build the other. They had the technology to do this, but now we have it too.'
– Mr Ifmail and Mr Mohamad, builders at KLCC.

THE PROTON CAR

Perusahaan Otomobil Nasional, or Proton, is a car that first appeared in 1985 in a joint project with the Japanese car manufacturers, Mitsubishi. Just ten years later, Proton controlled over 70 per cent of the domestic car market. This is partly because high import duties on foreign cars make Protons cheaper, but this no-nonsense car has also been successful overseas. In 1993, more than 17,000 Protons were exported to Britain. The car has also developed local engineering skills. From the very beginning, the number of foreign parts has been reduced by manufacturing these parts within Malaysia. The success of the 'First Nation Car Project' led to another. In 1994, Malaysia brought out a second, cheaper model, the Kancil.

Assembling cars in the Proton factory.

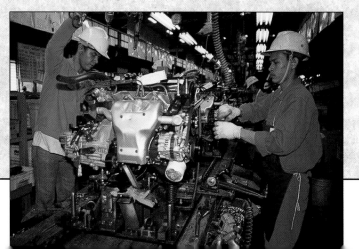

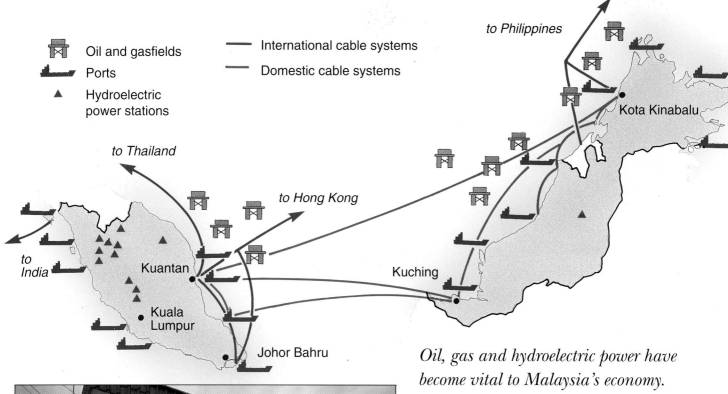

Oil and gasfields
Ports
Hydroelectric power stations
International cable systems
Domestic cable systems

to Philippines

Kota Kinabalu

to Thailand

to Hong Kong

to India

Kuantan

Kuala Lumpur

Kuching

Johor Bahru

Oil, gas and hydroelectric power have become vital to Malaysia's economy.

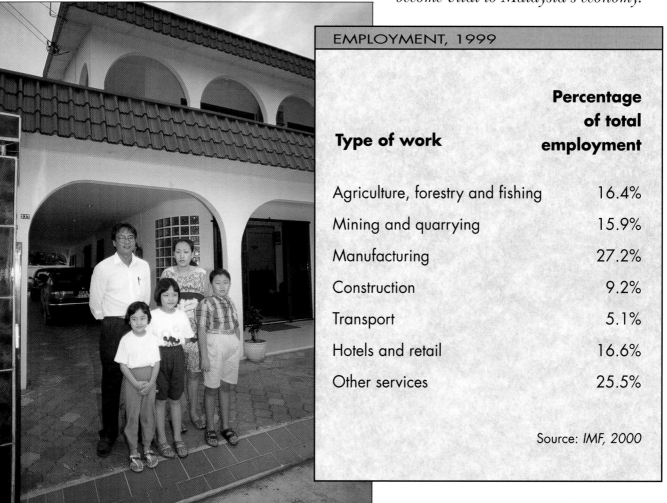

EMPLOYMENT, 1999

Type of work	Percentage of total employment
Agriculture, forestry and fishing	16.4%
Mining and quarrying	15.9%
Manufacturing	27.2%
Construction	9.2%
Transport	5.1%
Hotels and retail	16.6%
Other services	25.5%

Source: *IMF, 2000*

A Chinese family show off their new house, a sign of Malaysia's increasing wealth.

Leisure and tourism

FOREIGN TRAVEL

You only need to look at the travel shelves in your local bookshop or travel agent to see how important Malaysia is becoming as a tourist destination. It has taken the lead in South-east Asia for a variety of reasons. Resorts have grown around some of the many beaches, but others are still undeveloped. The mountains and hills, such as the Cameron Highlands, are ideal locations for hiking and activity holidays.

Rain forest parks and nature reserves serve two purposes in Malaysia: they protect the environment, enabling unique and rare species to survive in their natural habitats, and act as tourist attractions. Sepilok, a sanctuary near Sandakan, where orang-utans are reintroduced to the wild after periods in captivity, is one of the most famous examples.

Opposite Old and new are never far apart in Malaysia. On a beach in Penang modern tourist pursuits take place alongside traditional boats behind.

Below Modern hotels in Penang cater for wealthy foreign visitors to Malaysia.

Visitors who want to learn more about the culture of the indigenous groups can stay in longhouses in East Malaysia. Recently, there has also been an increase in international business conventions taking place in Malaysia. This means income not only for the convention centre, but for hotels, restaurants and tourist attractions.

Although it is Malaysia's third-biggest earner of foreign currency, tourism still remains a resource with a great deal of potential growth. Recently the government has promoted the country internationally by launching 'Visit Malaysia' years in 1990, 1994 and 1998. In 1998, Malaysia hosted the Commonwealth Games.

Tourism is important for the Malaysian economy. This tourist explains what she has learnt from her visit.

'We are really surprised by the amount of development in Malaysia. We hadn't expected such an organized country. When we told our friends we were going to Malaysia, no one had any idea what it would be like. There seems to be almost no information in Europe about this place, and everybody is so friendly.' – **Marion Esch, tourist from Germany (left).**

THE EASTERN AND ORIENTAL RAILWAY

In 1993, Orient Express Hotels launched a luxury train service between Singapore and Bangkok. Called the Eastern and Oriental (E&O) Express, it travels the 1,943 km journey through the Malay Peninsula in forty-two hours. With its wood-panelled interior, inspired by the 1932 film, *Shanghai Express*, it is aimed more at visitors than locals, although the passengers tend to be a mixture of wealthy Asians and Western honeymoon couples.

Inset The Genting Highlands resort is very modern inside and built to suit Western tastes.

Left A family of Indian Malays visits their local zoo for the day.

LOCAL TOURISM

As the Malaysian people have moved from the countryside to towns, their traditions have changed. Through better jobs, they now have more spare time and more money. This means that more Malaysians can now afford to take holidays. Local tourism has seen old hill stations, such as the Genting Highlands, converted into resorts that offer expensive hotels, golf courses, casinos and karaoke bars. Many Malaysians have no wish to leave their home comforts behind, so the resorts have recreated the luxuries of the city in the countryside.

41

LEISURE

Among young people, video games are popular, as are American films, which often appear many months before they are shown in Europe. Hamburger bars are places for the young to meet and relax. However, leisure time is often quite organized. Young Malaysians are encouraged to belong to groups and clubs, such as the Rakan Muda, that provide opportunities to experience the many outdoor activities of this beautiful country.

The one obsession that unites all of the population is badminton. Malaysians are among the best in the world at this sport. Soccer, basketball, table tennis, golf and squash are also popular sports.

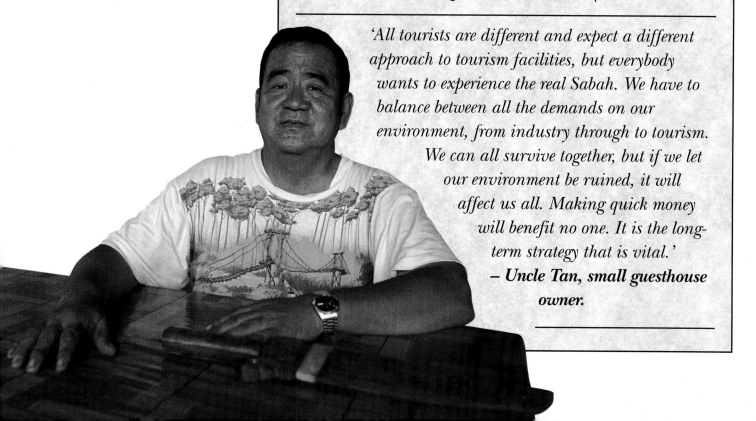

UNCLE TAN

Although tourism in eastern Sabah is still not well established, local business people are realizing its potential and are claiming exclusive rights to many places of interest. By building resorts that cater entirely for rich overseas visitors, they become too expensive for both locals and budget travellers. The island of Sipidan, which is considered one of the best scuba diving sites in the world, is an example.

Uncle Tan runs a guesthouse outside Sandakan. He still offers the chance to visit the offshore Turtle Islands, or spend time in a basic jungle camp, living amongst the proboscis monkeys, quite cheaply. But even Uncle Tan is finding it difficult to compete. The policy to encourage a more expensive type of tourism does not benefit the local economy as other kinds might. Besides, locals feel angry at not being able to afford to visit sights that were once open to all.

'All tourists are different and expect a different approach to tourism facilities, but everybody wants to experience the real Sabah. We have to balance between all the demands on our environment, from industry through to tourism. We can all survive together, but if we let our environment be ruined, it will affect us all. Making quick money will benefit no one. It is the long-term strategy that is vital.'
– Uncle Tan, small guesthouse owner.

One of the more popular tourist destinations is Langkawi Island, to the north-west of the peninsula.

PALAU LABUAN

Pulau Labuan, situated 10 km west of Sabah, in the South China Sea, is a strange place. It marks the point where tourism and economic development meet. Although it does not appear to be either tourist island or international offshore financial centre, it is both. The biggest attraction is its duty-free shopping, where people from Brunei, a nearby Islamic country, come to shop because alcohol is banned in their country. Yet it largely consists of buildings that are just two to four storeys high, with only limited international standard accommodation.

Night life is confined to a few pubs, discotheques and karaoke bars.

There are only two real tourist attractions – a Japanese war memorial which marks the point where their forces surrendered at the end of the Second World War, and the Chimney, which stands as a lasting memory of early industry based on coal. But all might change if the Malaysian government has its way. An exclusive 'financial park' is currently being built and it is hoped that it will turn the island into an offshore banking resort to rival Singapore and Hong Kong.

The future – 'Vision 2020'

The future of Malaysia looks bright. It has one of the fastest-growing economies of any Asian country. To keep this growth on target, Prime Minister Dr Mahathir has introduced a strategic plan called 'Vision 2020'. It is a plan that aims for full industrialization by the year 2020. Everywhere you go in Malaysia the idea is highlighted with banners and posters, and displayed on bridges and flower displays.

In April 1995, Dr Mahathir won the general election with more votes than ever. The prime minister himself is also popular. On National Day (*Merdeka*) or other special occasions, full-page adverts in the newspapers praise him as a champion of the Third World.

Above *Extra land for development has been reclaimed from the sea in Kota Kinabalu.*

AT HOME

This support allows the prime minister to press ahead with his grand plans. Having built the world's tallest flagpole in the capital, Kuala Lumpur, Dr Mahathir has his sights set on finishing the modern complex that contains the world's tallest building.

The government's building plans include the world's tallest hydroelectric dam at Bakun. In 1998, the new international airport opened at Sepang, together with a new sports complex for the Commonwealth Games.

The largest and most ambitious plan will give Malaysia a new administrative capital city. Called Putrajaya, and located 40 km south of Kuala Lumpur, the city will form a triangle with the new airport and current capital. Putrajaya will be a new 'mega-city, based upon satellite and multimedia technology.

An advertisement for the new airport at Sepang.

44

> *'Kuala Lumpur is going to see so much change in the next few years, with new developments on every side of the city. We are building low and high-rise apartments and small shops, which will provide for a whole new community, almost a new small town.'*
> **– *Joseph Khaw, architect.***

As development is not cheap, the government has cut costs by privatizing the main projects. For example, private companies have built the north-south highway and now charge a toll for vehicles on certain sections.

ABROAD

Dr Mahathir is becoming more respected. While the prime minister might appear quick to respond to criticism, he knows that Malaysia is now so important that it cannot be ignored.

The health of the financial centre appears to be strong. In the late 1990s, the Kuala Lumpur Stock Exchange (KLSE) went scripless (fully automated), which increased activity on the market.

Architects have the best view of what the future will look like in Malaysia. They are perhaps the most important people in the prime minister's 'Vision 2020'.

FURTHER DEVELOPMENT

According to Dr Mahathir, 'Malaysia is developing so rapidly that it has been recognized by international organizations as a model for developing countries.' But has the development been too fast? If labour wages keep rising, the Malaysians might price themselves out of the market. Foreign companies will then look for similar countries where both labour and land is cheaper. It is therefore essential that Malaysia carefully manages its further development in order to maintain its enormous success.

Glossary

Canopy The highest leafy layer in the rain forests.

Cash crops Crops that are produced for sale and not for personal use.

Colonial The people of a country who occupy and rule over another country.

Commodity Something that is produced using human labour.

Congestion Busy roads.

Deforestation A reduction in the area of land covered by trees.

Dialects Forms of a language that belong to specific groups of people.

Erosion Wearing away the land by natural agents such as wind or waves.

Ethnic The original people of a country.

Exploited Having made the maximum use of a resource.

Exports Products that a country sells abroad.

Humidity The degree of moisture in the air.

Hydroelectric Electric power that is produced by the energy of water.

Immigrants People who chose to move from their home country to another country.

Indigenous Originating naturally in a particular area (especially plants and wildlife) or, of people, being born in one region.

Industrialization The growth of large industries based on machines.

Infrastructure The framework or foundation of a country, such as transport and communications.

Integrated The successful mixing of an ethnic group into a society.

Manufacturing Making raw products into materials that can be sold.

Monarchy A state ruled by a king or a queen.

Primary production Industrial activity concerned with collecting or producing material that is natural, i.e. agriculture or mining.

Privatization The selling of, for example, companies that are publicly owned, to the private sector.

Reclaimed land Areas of land that were once underwater that have been taken back from the sea.

Resource Wealth supplied by nature, such as energy, minerals or timber.

Shifting cultivation A process by which land is cleared, cropped and then abandoned for another piece when the soil becomes exhausted.

Stock Exchange A trading place where people meet to buy and sell shares belonging to different companies.

Sustainable Something that can be maintained without reducing future levels.

Tropical A very hot, wet climate.

Urbanization A process involving the change of any area from countryside into towns.

Further information

Books to read

Continents: Asia by David Lambert (Hodder Wayland, 1997)
Discovering Malaysia by Richard Balkwill (Zoë Books, 1997)
Real World: South-East Asia by Anita Ganeri (Watts, 1995)

Addresses and websites

Asia Observer – Vietnam
Website: www.asiaobserver.com/malaysia.htm
News and background information on Malaysia.

Lonely Planet – Destination Malaysia
Website: www.lonelyplanet.com/destinations/south_east_asia/malaysia/
Good web pages on Malaysia.

Malaysia Tourism Promotion Board
57, Trafalgar Square, London WC2
Website: www.interknowledge.com/malaysia/
Background information about Malaysia, including a visit to a Borneo longhouse.

Malaysian High Commission
45 Belgravia Square, London SW1X 82J
The information library can provide facts about Malaysia, including a booklet,
Malaysia in Brief. Tel: 0207 919 0264

Index

Numbers in **bold** refer to illustrations.